ULTIMATUMS
Gordon Osing

Gordon

SPUYTEN DUYVIL
New York City

ISBN 978-1-944682-65-1

Cover picture , "A Break from Work," by Lewis Hine
(The Empire State Building Photographs, 1930-1931)
photographed by Cyd Fenwick

Library of Congress Cataloging-in-Publication Data

Names: Osing, Gordon, 1937- author.
Title: Ultimatums / Gordon Osing.
Description: New York City : Spuyten Duyvil, 2017.
Identifiers: LCCN 2017022190 | ISBN 9781944682651
Classification: LCC PS3565.S56 A6 2017b | DDC 811/.54--dc23
LC record available at https://lccn.loc.gov/2017022190

for my students over the years,
who endured with me the changing
stages of my learning

CONTENTS

"All he had to do was solve the mystery of the universe, which may be difficult but not as difficult as living an ordinary life."

Walker Percy, *Lancelot*

"We may sympathize intellectually with nothing else, but we certainly sympathize with our own selves."

Henri Bergson, *An Introduction to Metaphysics*

"One image crossed the many-headed, sat
Under the tropic shade, grew round and slow,
No Hamlet thin from eating flies, a fat
Dreamer of the Middle Ages. Empty eyeballs knew
That knowledge increases unreality, that
Mirror on mirror mirrored is all the show.
When gong and conch declare the hour to bless
Grimalkin crawls to Buddha's emptiness"

W. B. Yeats, "The Statues"

Our Cover Photo

I think I know this guy, I who couldn't
believe in the heights of words and
what follows, life on the straight and narrow,
in the beam of ruling, revealed language.
No Coptic I, hope necessarily bailed
before the divinity of words. The sky is
not where I figured to end up, singing
forever. I challenged fear in thin air.
I all but caught rivets in a bucket and
tossed them to the hammers and at lunch
sat and watched the clouds chase back
and forth always changing aspects. Look,
I moved deliberately or not at all.
Mine the Chinese mountain and the world
down there keeps doing, undoing itself
every moment all the time. The wind
carries and someone's shouts are the first
and last thing you hear on my ferris wheel.
Call it courage if you fancy that, but
Harold Lloyd hanging on the clock,
that's me. Up here any step is my last,
but I see the sky taking shape beneath me
and me up here in the sunlight that will
make it solid. People will shade their eyes
and stare up and sometimes shout, but I listen
for thunder and the wind changing directions.
And what do my eyes see but the towers
misted off to my left and right and behind me.
I listen with more than care to my world.
The hardest thing I do is traipse on land.

THE EYES HAVE IT

Who has not looked through a spyglass
backwards? The world is diminished so,
made for Lionel Train towns, far away
as beneath the feet everything, also
the diminished as if belonging to other
than yourself, not as if in a microscope,
thin to the eye on the stage barreling
not down but up (not breaking the stage)
and the mouth squinting or falling open
at the flowering in spirals of the stars,
the same infinitely out as in at Palomar,
and the stereopticon making art between
two not quite identical pictures of gardens,
the Isle of Capri, ancient Rome, the Leaning
Tower of Pisa, and the spinning crystals
bursting in the eye in the kaleidoscope.
All these machines made for the eye
define the eye by its gifts for distances,
alterations, and sciences of surveillance.
Look long enough and what does not change.
The eye is made for changes, detections.
There is even an eye looking into itself,
if you are lucky and have the habit of it.
If not you are already in a tumult of the self.
Contradictions, insolences to the ordinary: gold!
Who you gonna believe, me or your own eyes?

ONESELF VS. ONE'S SELF

"He who forms a tie is lost. The germ
of corruption has entered into his soul,"
wrote Joseph Conrad, so I'm lost,
having granted awareness to anyone
I think I'm talking to. I'm a youngest
and used to bargaining acceptance.
And I admit, the internal landscape
of another is deeper than a geography.
It is no small labor to understand
another. And one's self has to do it,
allowing oneself to become another,
as if it were a gift to depart the self,
a trick, or worse, a necessity born
of an original habit of abandonment.

What, another middle classer pretending
to a gift, or some leftover of survival
of another kind of pretending? A gift
in any case, seeing and hearing more
than the presented. Disallowing the presented
in fact in favor of one of its others,
assuming that disguises are ordinary
acting, in both senses, regular for life
and there are too many causes to count
to discount the insolences of heart, mind
and soul to the years, not to mention
the baroque gestures that make up
society, courtesies, indifferences, duties.
What all doesn't anybody know in secret.

It's the sort of stuff that ghosts fiction,
that deepens scenes, invents reflection,
that causes the invented to resemble life.
It's the unsettled quality in a writer's
being that makes him (or her) an author.
A hard way to live disbelieving oneself
is the author's fate, alone by the lamp,
guessing, speaking tries to one's self,
allowing one thing to invent another,
arriving where one did not know before,
seeing the least changes invent others,
even abandoning moments of language
and moving on in momentary uncertainty.
It's lucky the consolations in it are addictive.

SEPTEMBER 9TH, MOMENTS IN THE DAO

—the Double Ninth Festival in China

1.
Iridescent blue butterfly
disappears one with frog's green lip-
flapping tongue magic.

2.
Leaves shoot nevertheless
from a floating log blown into shore
where I had thought to rest.

3.
Rasping moccasin swirls silver-dark
in the eye following the cove's shoreline
beneath the planks of the reading dock.

4.
The far boat dock, sunlit,
turns into a stage a nameless day,
and the lake to a wild boy-smell.

5.
Noon's sunlit racing waves
go under the swimming dock and never
to any increase of light.

6.
The Autumn moon in daylight:
the Dowager Empress' veil, or else a letter
lost from language, seemingly seen through.

7.
Near is far as far is near,
shouting and whispering good as the same
for once eye's opinion.

8.
Bluejay's fine print, noted, says:
let only one of the cats be God, and
therefore second chances the truth.

9.
Late, neither night nor morning,
venomed fear eases the eye's steps artfully.
Who would want a harmless Paradise.

REPROACH

Censure is far too polite a word for it.
Disgrace, ignominy, rebuke, and shame
are better, if indignity in the aftermath
is to be imagined, a two edged blade
in that it has to be accepted or outlived.
It would be like having to invent love
where none was, and that invention has
to find a theatre, a form for translation
of an abandoned self, similar to the one
described in the New Testament. Remember?
Elijah and Moses summoned from their cloud,
and you know who stands between them.
Ibsen and Albee would be just as good
if it had to be, and it did.

One writes in the absurd life,
the fictive life, in Nemerov's phrase,
that didn't need to be but is
the only way, as luck would have it.
But how to make the fictive engaging
is a matter of facility for the mind
making it up good enough to be true,
better even because more nuanced
with the ways long since traditions,
ditties, songs, and yes, poetry. Touching
bottom in the heart, a further *felix culpa*
than the one taught in seminaries, *ergo*
is mercy to the life chosen and gamboled.
Lucky's the driven from the harsh Garden of creeds.

In Conclusion

Gravity is not my friend tonight.
Sput is, however, if it means anything,
and I'm not entirely sure I am destined
to definitions. We are skiing an avalanche.
(Funnier as thought, of course.) We
are accelerated in time and intimacies
within our worlds. It is not possible
to speak of ends, reasons or certainties.
The truth does well to live three days,
called a news-span I believe. Besides
"Nobody ever went broke underestimating
the American people," Henry Mencken said.
Living in the "now" v. living the past:
I say back and forth is the way to go.

The burdens of prejudice locked in time
are many. False dilemmas all over the place
are many. But what does the glance know
that time does not, and vice versa. Either
can come to love and either to the other.
Dante and Othello are witnesses here,
one seeing her briefly then always,
the other strangling her the rest of his life.
Sans mulling, and thereafter I desire
to become this game of meters and arguments,
and to play it without too much forethought,
if you see what I mean. I want to think
in the old forms conjuring the arguments.
Let the best guesses take me where they will.

Reruns

I see on the telly directory the same
movies run for weeks and months,
which invites a disquisition on how
people see them over and over, like
other stuff one could name, monotonous
church services, football reruns, scenes
on the news. I mean what is the charge
in watching guaranteed outcomes all
the way to becoming eyes' final takes
repeatedly. I know, we used to go
into the movies in the middle and stay
until the middle became the beginning,
but not the same movie five times.
So why see a movie endlessly?

You know what is coming and what
has come before. What is confirmed
by repetition? Motives, clues, gestures
that prove acting? The meanings altered
in the screen, their consolations, to permanence?
Their inevitabilities, comforting determinations?
Their certainties of acting in identical moments?
Their guarantees of characters' apparent decisions?
Let us imagine none and all of the above.
Secretly we see ourselves seeing, and are
comforted not having to worry about
the outcome, the appearances of both folly and
the tragic, and it is to escape both we watch,
comforted nothing in our world is overturned.

MAYBE SCHEHEREZADE

You have heard likely about Scheherazade,
who made up stories for the Sultan to save
her own life, night after night, because
his custom was to have her and then
have her killed so he would be the only
one she ever had. This is, I suppose,
the origin of The Divine Right of Kings.
You may even have been treated by
Rimsky-Korsakov's slithering musical
settings of the tone of that wise gal's
knack for saving her skin from the knife
with stories. Let me tell you her plight
is all but universal. A good story can
and does keep the old mill running
in the eye of the mind for a while,
and that while means you're paying
attention to see where and how it ends,
and so the ultimate silence is averted.

Speaking of which, I am delighted to be
speaking about it not yet in the third
person. I have begun many a piece without
knowing where it would end and I like
artificial endings, even if they are only
language. They kept the plates spinning,
the pins in the air. You know what I mean.

The beginning is a first clue to endings,
I'll tell you that much. Reversals, switches,
figurative shifts, even lowly puns work,
and suggestions for the next night especially
will do. Notes for one piece call to light
another. The listener in mind is aging too,
which evens the odds of survival a little.
And what choice is there? The long and short
haul are the same. Dalliances are precious
either way. Death doesn't fool around.
He'll see you in Samara on his day.
But he likes a good story. That's his flaw,
so start noticing. Pick up on contradictions,
unsolvable mysteries, riddles, open questions,
above all opposition to whatever orthodoxies.
Consort with your only soul for beginnings.

Heaven

Heaven is always opposite worlds,
escape from pain to believers in the *Medium Aevum*,
a garden of flowers to chimneyed Victorians,
a second chance with separated loved ones,
or eternal singing before brilliant light
to those who got past Tin Pan Alley.
Heaven is always an other, it seems to me,
a pure and final out of what is left behind,
ours a golden age in a culture forced
to abandon their past by the conquering faith
of a Mediterranean religion. Our culture
seems to get by, though, on the ambiguous
that lets everyone invent his own idea
of what world he is saved in after words.

Even coitus does, or favorite last meals,
or living and breathing as usual but
within a sky filled with Mozart, Bach
and Brahms's sweetly remembering
how it was in fields of early Autumn,
savoring turned earth and burned fields,
and a first chill of Winter, the sublime ending
of the day that will follow, not yet freezing.
The scent will endure and the body will
be alive to know in this time this world
is Heaven as in the endless devices of music,
wordless hyperboles made for human instruments
and performances, invitations to live more
truly in the fictional conjurings of music.

LYING

> "There is no document of civilization that is not
> at the same time a document of barbarism."
> —Walter Benjamin

So what is it that amazes me even now?
Dissembling, exaggerating, minimizing, shading
what is in the moment taken for truth: I was,
am, good at it, so good I am aware I might
be doing it virtually all of the time. Mindful
I am of the inherent prevarication of the said
in words, which already invent translations
in time, from moment to scene in the mind.
I mean why should I be so tender about my
instantaneous guardings of my self when,
in Benjamin's declaration, plus Freud's
by the way, the whole shebang is founded
on self-deceptions and monstrous fabrications.
My self a fiction were not too bold a try.

But it is the speed, the automaticity (I
know, there is no such word.) with
which I respond to a lead that amazes.
I hardly have to think about it. I seem
to have calculated a good deal about
both the moment and also the other,
the whole presence of a listener's interest.
What could inspire such a need for
self-protection. It is a redoubtable
talent in my service, yes. but also
a case of moral ambiguity. It is
a lifetime of responding that has been
my fate, a version of fear my reason.
Truth is, I was born to learn lying.

So what! What language will we speak
in heaven? What words parting the clouds
on the way up. What does Antaeus' story
teach us about our soundings and our
realized moments in a world. We imagine
with past days and hours, places and sayings,
none particularly true except in the moment
of saying. Then everything is invested,
ourselves, the listener, both our pasts,
even reasons deeply hidden to both of us.
We may as well say talk is theatre
with all the lights on. Heaven, if it is,
is theatre the actors translated. Truth to tell
nobody knows anything more than that.

POETRY

I love it, language cut loose from
moments and objects, sentences entirely
about a fictive self remembering its own
fictivity, like a Magritte's painter looking
at his painting outside the window the wall,
outdoors surrounding inside. The writer may
very well be hiding within the work
that he is causing you to reenact. His
is the artifact that lives by its own
principles, separate from its cause
that has become its model. Language
in mid-air, on the high wire, suspended.
Decadent by reason of a luxury in saying
that often enough abjures its causes.

Pretextualize (another made-up word),
the mind of the body of the maker
asks its founding moment to step aside,
having no reason to intrude on the result,
subsequently raised, like a chalice, over
the aliment, comprising nourishment you
can't see, but think about long after.
I think I just named trans-substantiation
as the chemistry of the heart and soul,
unless I con your imagination. (Perish
the thought.) You'd think I had a thing
about ecclesias, and this not the first time
matters of a faith intruded into a secular art.

What is Longinus' sublime but a shade
of an after-life, and isn't Heaven like
a Golden Age, as in China, only it's ahead
instead of held in the ancient village order,
and Shelley's "unacknowledged legislation"
something like canon law, only lodged
in spiritistic faith in Antaeus' ordinary lives.
The past is very close I tell you,
and you pray to it as to a divinity,
to find yourself blessed in it, because
for a very long time, and you'll have
some 'splaining to do to the gone,
Shinto-wise. In other words beware
of one who declares one life to be enough.

ULTIMATUMS

"I ain't gonna tell you again."

How often did we hear this from Mother,
meaning a last warning before whatever
worse things will be inflicted on you.
We heard it a thousand times, almost
every time, often enough in fact, that
we were forced to consider how terribly bad
the promised punishment could be, and so
it lost its value to us as threatening.
It declined in value, like Italian *lira*,
though our fear of her dark countenance
and abject anger counseled our empathy
for her stuck at home with three boys
and father, a travelling auditor gone.
I say it now to toilets and broken hoses.

The sheep that cried wolf comes to mind,
and I wonder if anyone escapes warning.
We were known to smile at its disaster
promised. There was enough in our home.
She was an angry woman. No childhood.
Fear and shame any day, for any reason.
She could be knives and frozen brown eyes,
cold in the arms, out of control at heart.
It were criminal not to forgive such a one,
and we were chary boys. I think of her
when I speak the phrase even now.
It is re-coded for the smile in it, finally.
Learning to become my words saved me.
Smile with me while there is still time.

WHAT THOSE WOMEN KNEW

To remember feelings is to create them,
to invite them to enter the body and to narrate
their materiality, to image them to silent music
no one can hear unless risking the roar
that lies at the heart of silence, George Eliot's
revelation and Jane Austen's deliberate phrase,
"the beast of mind." What did those women
know that is that monster under the bed,
fierce eyes in the closet, motion in the dark hall
wavering in the moonlight? The last feeling
one may have is mixed fear and anger,
and even impossible realizations of other
worlds to come, promised and so trusted.
They knew the beast of the earth is love.

THE PERIL

What is conviction to performance? Sure,
Luther devalued James's letter as "an Epistle
of straw" for its valuing of works along-
side faith, "which the just shall live by,"
I know, "*sola fide*" and all that. But
what about Phillipe Petit, who walked
on a rope between the Twin Towers.
(My student insisted he practiced a lot.)
And, again, our cover shot of the laborer
on break on the Rockefeller Center under
construction, having a smoke, looking
around at the traffic of lives. What do
these men have that eclipses mere
visionary certainty? Their practice is
a form of madness is it not? How
does one forget the balances it takes
to live every day in the ordinary world?
That is a kind of madness, too. What
holds your life together, friend? Likely
enough, but not without its madness
at the core, its quality as a living dream.
You think you cannot fail? Move
one block over and see what Hawthorne's
"Wakefield" saw, you a stranger to yourself,
seeing things as unfamiliar, not knowing
what beloveds are looking at and thinking,
and how life goes on without you or them.
The narrowest beam of life is everything.

LEFTOVERS

We had them mostly Sunday evenings,
along with Gene Autry's "Melody Ranch,"
"Sam Spade," and "Jack Benny," "Amateur Hour."
Anything in the fridge was game for a meal
and Sunday's dinner, relived, made the best.
We ate cold food easy as a Chinese Festival.
Father went down to a sleeper car parked
on a Depot siding, to be in Chicago the next
morning to begin the audit. He stayed
at the Atlantic (salesman) Hotel generally.

I walked home nice afternoons, behind
the C & A freight house (later the G M & O),
past the Meadowgold Dairy for ice cream,
over the viaduct on Fourth Street. Watch,
but better, listen for the three o'clock
down from Chicago, Number Five
I think it was. You named trains for
the minute they are supposed to arrive
unless they had a famous name. Numbers
two and four, the Abe Lincoln, the Ann Rutledge.
I worked night clerk in the baggage room
in both Springfield and Lincoln. Sort of
invited to leave college, I was that year.
I think I was too lonesome to obey rules.
I guess I didn't need the authority of the cloth.
Plus, a girl could drive me mad with sacrifice
and some did. And now I am a leftover
myself, and just maybe part *farouche,* too.
Insolence often as not seemed right to me.
I can't tell you why while I am writing this.

LEVIATHON

It is in consultations with the body
that I learned the other world I had
lived in all along but didn't know.
The body's less than secret witness
revealed how marginal were the generalities
openly honored, but privately offering
other presentations. Watch for the evidence
of other ways to see, hear, feel, etcetera,
like in the joke with a substitute, surprising,
right ending, that both finishes and changes
the information in the story, amounts to
insolence to the ordinary, very much like
a joke. Poetry and comedy have something
in common, They change the terms of knowing.

Leviathon is the word of the world, that feeds,
like Jonah's beast, on needs to escape, and sets
competitions in belonging as the measures of
humor, acquisitions, fear, vanity and obituaries.
They call it "cross-talk" in China, comics
misusing words, an amusement at inferior
understanding on the night train, our ads for
right goods everywhere, needing to fit in
and the crucial submissions one has to acquire
to nobody's language, having no world
before Gutenberg. Pity us all our devotion
to Leviathon, who can't get back to the grace
of community, and community is everything.
The comedy of salvation requires defying time.

A Woods Bell

> "…tone
> which like a deeper ear
> hears us, seeming hearers."
>
> —Rilke, "Gong"

On Koh Samui in Thailand I remember
one day wandering in the island forest
coming to a woods bell and living
a while in its sound.

1.
I regret most the stampede of years,
then that a true body of the heart
can never be whole, not even
so much as abandoned geographies
that have repaired themselves in time.
I want stations of the hours. My Dao
in the Blues has brought me here,
who knows if finally or for a while.

What I lack at home is a woods bell
to ring randomly and not the hours,
to unite the silences, to prove the moments
the solid matters of intervals, pealing
the skin off time like an orange,
to make it whole any moment for a while.

To make time whole the way the sea
in all its roiling up
every rhythm of waters at once
yet shapes the shell
to a fine intricacy.

What is needed at home is a woods bell,
for its summary calling down
all time as endless in every part.
These woods have needed for a long time
to be made one. Even now
I see the sparkling lake coming toward me
that never can arrive, but never mind.
One envies poems though which of them
was ever finished.

A bell hollows out time. One sees time.
It sounds and the jungle is a garden,
wild as God, is there an eternal while
in its tone declining.

2.
Do not worry about the sound declining,
as if going away, finally the silences.
The very letters of your name began in stone.
Quit expecting what does not exist,
declining what does. Therefore a bell,
nature's only pure sound...

that parses time, is all intervals at once
and none, rings on and on echoing
life for a while, and then is never
truly gone, not merely a sullen carnival
of singing stone, but time turned
to a ringing at the center of the mind,
amazed and whole, visible circles of time
rising outward from where the heart's stone
is cast in circles ringing in the mind.

I will yet satisfy my house
with some raw glorying in iron,
earth's mutest metal for celebration.
I will have a bell to cancel the hours
of nameless days, taken up evenings,
sounding from time to time, randomly,
whelming the insects' waves of screeching
in darkness erasing everything.

ARCHAEOLOGY

Never having lived beyond their own
changeable utilities they elaborated
the hypothesis that they need never die.
They took language itself for eternal life.

All that remained of their heathen past
was an insignificant reservation,
sincerity explicitly forbidden secretly
unless temporary and a matter of laughter.

Love was the loss in which something
could be made perfect, their deepest
faith was. Beast-angels, angel-beasts:
how should they begin to prove which.

Like deities, they squandered what they loved.
Hearts migrated to worlds forbidden to eyes.

Made in the USA
Lexington, KY
11 May 2017